Things I couldn't say

Charlie Mihalop

BookLeaf
Publishing
India | USA | UK

Presentation by *BookLeaf Publishing*

Web: www.bookleafpub.com

E-mail: info@bookleafpub.com

ISBN: 9789357447270

First edition 2022

DEDICATION

This book is dedicated to my Mum who has been my guide through the darkest days and Winnie who taught me how to love.

My Defects

Under this sun, it was always you
The problem was my love, you were my equal.
I wasn't strong enough to withstand your
intellect
I needed imperfections, weaknesses
I needed to feel godly but I did not
You were too complete
For my broken soul.

Veil

For as long as I can remember
I've been trying to work out
How to be me in company.
Are we ever who we really are when we're not
alone?

Gratitude

On this journey, I found a power greater than
myself
I learnt the meaning of humility
The value of distance from inauthentic energy
Sobriety was the greatest gift I ever allowed
myself to accept.

Secret Place

My heart is full
But there's a hole in my soul
I don't need you to fill it
Just find it
I'll meet you there.

HP

All glory to her who calms me
When I cannot ground myself
A whispering wind when I would feel fury
A contentment I've never known.

Champ

This mind of mine is deeper
Than most people care to swim
But you came equipped with a regulator
For that, you will never be unloved by me.

Escape Route

There isn't a drug in the world
That can make life meaningful
But are we searching for meaning
Or can we settle for being numb?
Living in the problem is hard
Sometimes reality is harder
So we run
I'm not saying it's right
I'm saying I understand.

Next

Raw emotions flooded my insides
As I watched her drive away
There goes my world again
What's next?
Burn the whole place down
& watch the stars cry.

Love Affair

Go. But go softly
Go everywhere with love
Let love be the beginning
The middle
And the end.

Hesitance

Be a mind that is sure
In a crowd full of doubt.

LOUDER

PLEASE DONT RETREAT
DO NOT DEFLATE OR DECREASE
DONT LIVE TO PLEASE OR APPEASE
For you are extraordinary.

Inspired

I noticed her without realising
Her passion ran through me
Unblocked my will and my words
Embrace the unfamiliar woman
She could be your muse.

If we're being honest

I was comforted by your contradictions
& committed to your lies
It's funny, you taught me so much about love
For someone who never really loved me.

Yours

You are yours before you are ever anyone else's
I don't wish to own you, but I'd give thanks to
god a thousand times over to hold your hand
through the madness
Feeling full and lonely, together.

& now I'm lukewarm

When I said you were beautiful
What I really meant was:
I love the way you feel like sunlight
You warm me all the way through.

Persistence

I knew she wasn't you from the beginning
Not even close to everything you'll be
Her touch didn't feel like home
Her eyes never really saw me

With you I'll be awake
You'll speak to me in a language I've not yet
heard but somehow understand
You will be more than everything
So I'll wait.

Poison

There I was, defeated and resentful
Full of chaos, no direction
You found me and filled me up
I will always remember
How you made me smile
Right before you brought me to my knees.

Letting go

I hope now to understand
More than to be understood
To be motivated by love
Rather than fear
I pray to accept
Over fighting to be right.
I'm finally paying attention.

www.ingramcontent.com/pod-product-compliance
Lightning Source LLC
LaVergne TN
LVHW041303200726
843507LV00014B/3115